The Tiny Book of Boss Jokes

GW00383050

In This Series

The Tiny Book of Dirty Jokes
The Tiny Book of Dirty Limericks
The Tiny Book of Drinking Jokes
The Tiny Book of Football Jokes
The Tiny Book of Golf Jokes
The Tiny Book of Irish Jokes
The Tiny Book of Lawyer Jokes
The Tiny Book of Marriage Jokes
The Tiny Book of Men Jokes
The Tiny Book of Rugby Jokes
The Tiny Book of Scottish Jokes
The Tiny Book of Women Jokes

The Tiny Book of Boss Jokes

Edward Phillips

Illustrated by
Noel Ford

HarperCollins*Publishers*

HarperCollins*Publishers*
77–85 Fulham Palace Road,
Hammersmith, London W6 8JB

www.**fire**and**water**.com

This paperback edition 2002
1 3 5 7 9 8 6 4 2

Previously published by
HarperCollins*Publishers* 1994

ISBN 0 00 715260 4

Set in Stone Sans by Rowland Phototypesetting Ltd,
Bury St Edmunds, Suffolk
Printed in Great Britain by BemroseBooth Ltd

The little office clerk crept meekly into the boss's office. 'Excuse me, sir,' he said. 'I'm sorry to bother you, but my wife told me that I had to ask you for a raise.'

'I see,' said the boss. 'All right – I'll ask my wife if I can give you one.'

'Will you ever forget that lovely weekend we had together on the French Riviera?' the boss asked his beautiful secretary.

'What's it's worth?' she said slyly.

The boss was addressing a meeting of the firm's senior executives and sales staff. 'Now, when my son starts work here on Monday morning,' he said, 'I want you to treat him just as you would treat any other new employee who was going to take over the company in two years' time.'

'Briggs,' said the boss one morning, 'I just don't know how we're going to get along without you – but starting Monday, we're going to try.'

The managing director of a merchant banker's firm in the City recently circulated the following memo to all staff:

I am instituting a new system in the company which we shall refer to as the Work Period. I am asking that all employees will endeavour to find some time during the day to implement Work Periods – without, of course, infringing on coffee breaks, lunch hours, rest periods, selling raffle tickets, taking up office collections and planning holidays.

Said the foreman of a lumber company to an applicant for a tree-felling job: 'Where did you learn to chop down trees?'

'In the Sahara,' said the lad.

'The Sahara? There are no trees in the Sahara!'

'No,' said the lad. 'Not now there aren't.'

A new chauffeur for the managing director reported for work one Monday morning. As the boss climbed into the back of the Rolls-Royce, he said, 'What's your name, driver?'

'Henry, sir,' said the chauffeur.

'I don't call my chauffeur by his Christian name,' said the boss huffily. 'What's your surname?'

'Darling, sir.'

'Very well then, Henry – drive on,' said the boss.

The boss called his top executive into his office and said, 'Wilkins, I've been watching you carefully over the last few months. You're hard-working, industrious, efficient – and you've made it your business to find out everything about the company's affairs, down to the smallest detail. Consequently, you're fired. It's men like you who resign and go off to start rival companies!'

The manager called his assistant into the office and closed the door sternly. 'Now listen to me,' he said. 'There's £50 missing from the petty cash box. There are only two keys to that box. I have one and you have the other.'

'Well,' said the assistant, 'suppose we each put in £25 and say no more about it?'

The boss had been married just over a year. Now he stood in the bedroom gazing down in wonder at the cot where his new baby son lay sleeping peacefully. 'A penny for your thoughts, dear,' said his wife in a soft voice.

'I was just wondering,' said the boss, 'how on earth they can turn out a cot like that for only £49.50!'

A pretty young secretary walked into her boss's office one morning and said, 'I've got some good news and some bad news.'

'Look, I'm very busy this morning,' said the boss. 'I haven't got time to mess about – just tell me the good news.'

'Well,' said his secretary, 'the good news is that you're not sterile.'

A top executive has been defined as a man who can take as long as he wants to make a snap decision.

Remember, the boss is not always right; but he is always the boss.

SECRETARY: 'Excuse me, sir, I think you're wanted on the phone.'

BOSS: 'What do you mean "you think" I'm wanted on the phone? Either I am or I'm not!'

SECRETARY: 'Well, sir, the caller said, "Is that stupid old idiot in yet?"'

It was the annual general meeting and the managing director was in the middle of his opening address when the door opened and his secretary came in with a worried look on her face. 'Excuse me, sir,' she whispered, 'the treasurer wants to give his report. He's calling long distance.'

The boss was interviewing a new secretary. 'What sort of salary were you expecting?' he asked.

'About £200 a week,' replied the girl.

'£200?' said the boss with a smile. 'I'll give you that with pleasure.'

'With pleasure,' she said, 'it'll be £500 a week.'

The boss came storming out of his office in a rage. 'There are too many telephones on my desk!' he shouted. 'I've just been speaking to myself for the last five minutes!'

FIRST BOSS: 'How's your new secretary shaping up?'

SECOND BOSS: 'She's incredible! She's only been with us a week and already she's a month behind in her work!'

Personnel manager to job applicant: 'What we're looking for is a man with initiative, drive, enthusiasm and determination. A man with leadership qualities; a man who can inspire others. In short, a man who can pull the company's darts team up from the bottom of the league.'

The boss was saying goodbye to his secretary. 'I'll be sorry to lose you,' he said. 'You've been just like a daughter to me – rude, surly, bad-mannered and lazy.'

Just for a change, why don't you go in to work tomorrow, say, 'Good morning' to the time clock, and punch your boss?

Two office girls were discussing their boss. 'Isn't he wonderful?' enthused the first. 'And doesn't he dress well?'

'Yes,' replied the second. 'And so quickly too!'

FIRST BUSINESSMAN: 'I really can't understand why your business failed.'

SECOND BUSINESSMAN: 'Too much advertising.'

FIRST BUSINESSMAN: 'Oh, come on – you never spent a penny on advertising.'

SECOND BUSINESSMAN: 'No – but my competitors did.'

The boss listened sympathetically as one of his young executives explained why he needed a raise. 'Yes, I quite understand,' said the boss. 'I realize you can't get married on the salary I'm paying you – and some day, believe me, you'll thank me for it.'

'What are you doing on Sunday night?' the boss asked his attractive young secretary.

'Nothing, sir,' she said hopefully.

'Good,' said the boss. 'In that case, try to get in on time on Monday morning.'

Boss: 'What's worrying you, Palmer?'

Employee: 'Automation, sir. I'm afraid I'm going to be replaced by a machine.'

Boss: 'Don't worry. They haven't invented a machine yet that does absolutely nothing!'

The personnel manager of a large car works in the Midlands received a questionnaire from the Department of Industry. One of the questions was: 'How many employees do you have, broken down by sex?' He replied: 'With us, alcohol is more of a problem.'

A new secretary started work on Monday morning and the boss, who was a stickler for detail, said, 'Now, Miss Haines, I can't stress too highly the importance of punctuation.'

'I understand, sir,' said the secretary. 'Don't worry. I always get to work on time.'

The boss was interviewing a young lady for the post of secretary. 'How many words a minute can you type?' he asked.

'Long ones or short ones?' she queried.

The managing director of a large firm had a huge sign made up which said in bold letters: DO IT NOW! Within a week three employees had asked for a raise, the assistant manager had run off with the boss's secretary, six typists had left to get married and the chief accountant had absconded with £50,000.

'Anything interesting happen at the office, dear?' asked the wife of a company manager as her husband returned home from the office one evening.

'Well,' he replied, 'I took one of those Aptitude Tests this afternoon and all I can say is – thank God I own the company!'

Many bosses believe in the theory of reincarnation. It's not surprising really because they see it demonstrated every day at five o'clock when their employees come alive to go home.

'Definitely not!' said the boss. 'I most certainly cannot let you have two hours off for lunch. If I did that, I'd have to do the same for every employee whose wife had just had triplets!'

The managing director of an insurance firm was visiting one of his subordinates who was ill in hospital. 'Don't worry about the office, Jack,' he said consolingly. 'Everybody's going to pitch in and do your work – as soon as we can find out just what it is you've been doing.'

A boss has been described as a man who comes in to work late when you're early, and then comes in early when you're late.

A lot of people who think their boss is stupid would be out of a job if he were any smarter.

Employee: 'Excuse me, sir, I've been working here for ten years and since I'm doing the work of three men, I feel I'm entitled to a raise.'

Boss: 'Well, I can't give you a raise but if you tell me the names of the other two men, I'll fire them.'

As the office boy strolled in half an hour late, the boss said, 'You should have been here at nine o'clock!'

'Why?' said the office boy. 'What happened?'

'You look worried, boss. Is anything wrong?' asked the secretary.

'Wrong?' said the boss. 'I have so many worries that if something catastrophic happened today, I wouldn't have time to worry about it until next week!'

The chairman of the board was reading the story of Cinderella to his small son. The boy was particularly interested in the part of the story which described how the pumpkin turned into a golden coach. 'Dad,' he asked, 'did Cinderella have to declare the coach as earned income or could she write it off as capital gain?'

The owner of a large factory offered a reward of £100 for the best money-saving suggestion submitted by an employee. The first prize was won by one of the workers who suggested that the reward should be reduced to £50.

The millionaire head of a large multinational was lunching with a friend. 'Why do you continue to work so hard?' asked his friend. 'Surely you've made enough money by now to be able to take things easy?'

'I'm just curious, that's all,' said the tycoon. 'I want to find out if there's any income my wife can't live beyond.'

FIRST SECRETARY: 'How is your boss to work for?'

SECOND SECRETARY: 'He's very bigoted.'

FIRST SECRETARY: 'In what way?'

SECOND SECRETARY: 'He thinks words can only be spelled one way.'

When the boss came into the office fifteen minutes early one morning, he surprised the office manager locked in a fond embrace with his personal secretary. 'Jones!' thundered the boss. 'You're not paid to do this, you know!'

'I know, sir,' said Jones. 'But I don't mind.'

'Get the telephone, Miss Summers,' said the boss irritably to his new secretary. 'I do wish you'd answer it when it rings.'

'There doesn't seem to be much point,' said his secretary. 'Nine times out of ten, it's for you!'

OFFICE BOY: 'I feel like telling the boss what I think of him again!'

SALES CLERK: 'What do you mean – again?'

OFFICE BOY: 'I felt like it yesterday too!'

'How's that new secretary of yours getting along?' one boss asked another as they were lunching at their club.

'She's either very stupid or very clever,' said his colleague. 'She's only been with me a week, but she's already got things in such a mess that I can't get along without her.'

The boss was furious. 'Wilkinson!' he thundered. 'Come in here at once! What's this I hear about you praying in church last Sunday for a raise? You know I can't stand people going over my head!'

'Is it true that your boss is going to make you a partner?'

'Yes, I think so. He said yesterday, "Either you take an interest in the business, or you get out!"'

'Boss,' said the foreman on a building site, 'the shovels haven't arrived. What shall we do?'

'Tell the men to lean on each other,' said the boss.

In desperation, the boss of a large manufacturing company put up a big sign in the machine shop. It read: 'This is a non-profit organization. Please help us change!'

BOSS: 'You're an hour late! Where have you been?'

CLERK: 'Having my hair cut.'

BOSS: 'What! On company time?'

CLERK: 'Well, it grew on company time.'

BOSS: 'It didn't all grow on company time!'

CLERK: 'Well, I didn't have it all cut off.'

Down-at-heel boss to bank manager: 'How do I stand for a loan?'

Bank manager: 'You don't – you grovel.'

The Boss's Prayer: 'O, Lord, let me be Thy servant. Show me what to do. Guide me to my duty. Give me work to do – but, o Lord, let it be in an advisory capacity.'

BOSS: 'Sanders, you've been drinking! I can smell it on your breath!'

SANDERS: 'Yes, sir! I've been celebrating the tenth anniversary of the last time you gave me a raise.'

The chairman of the board had to make a speech at an important function. He was very nervous about this and as the moment drew near for him to speak, the toastmaster didn't help matters by whispering to him, 'Are you ready to speak now, sir – or shall we let them enjoy themselves for a little longer?'

SALESMAN: 'I've been trying for three days to see you, sir. Have you got a minute to spare?'

BUSY BOSS: 'Arrange a date with my secretary.'

SALESMAN: 'I did, sir, and we had a wonderful time – but I'd still like to see you.'

'You're looking worried, dear,' said the wife of a top executive one night at dinner. 'Is anything wrong?'

'Nothing at all,' said the boss. 'I'm very optimistic about the future of the company.'

'Then why are you looking so anxious?' asked his wife.

'Because I'm not sure my optimism is justified!'

'My boy,' said the boss to his son, 'if you ever have the misfortune to be declared bankrupt, always travel first class. That way you'll never bump into one of your creditors.'

It has been said that a business conference of top executives is like the mating of elephants. It takes place at a high level, it involves a lot of labour and it produces nothing for two years.

The boss had been away on business for several days. Shortly after he returned home, the telephone rang one evening. He answered it and then hung up. 'Who was that, dear?' asked his wife.

'It was a wrong number,' said the boss. 'Some fellow wanted to know if the coast was clear so I put him on to the Meteorological Office.'

'Chief,' said the office manager to the boss one morning, 'I'm afraid we're going to have to get rid of that new office boy. Whenever I give him a job to do, he gets someone else to do it for him. He's lazy.'

'That's not laziness,' said the boss. 'That's executive ability!'

'As you enter the world of commerce,' said the millionaire business tycoon to his son, 'I want you to bear one thing in mind: money isn't everything. A man with one million pounds can be just as happy as a man with ten million.'

'Good news, dear,' said the boss when he arrived home from the office. 'I've at last managed to land that big government contract!'

'Honestly?' said his delighted wife.

'Let's not go into that now,' the boss frowned.

'What do you want a raise for?' asked the managing director.

'Well, sir,' said the junior, 'it's just that my kids have been pestering me ever since they found that their friends' families eat three meals a day.'

The boss had told his wife never to ring him at the office unless is was urgent, so he was rather annoyed when she telephoned one day to say that there was something wrong with the car. 'What's the matter with it?' he said irritably.

'Well, dear,' she said, 'I think the engine's flooded.'

'All right, I'll take a look at it when I get home,' said the boss. 'Where is the car now?'

'In the canal,' said his wife.

The boss's secretary was leaving to get married and the boss had taken up a collection amongst the staff and bought her a leaving present. 'Where can we hide it until the presentation?' asked the assistant manager.

'Put it in the filing cabinet,' said the boss. 'She never could find anything in there.'

At the annual shareholders' meeting, the chairman of the board was coming under attack from the dissatisfied stockholders who suspected him of engaging in fraudulent dealings with a government department. One shareholder stood up and shouted, 'I demand that you reveal the name of the sinister interest that controls you!'

'You leave my wife out of this!' the chairman shouted back.

Boss: 'Now, Wilkinson, we are giving you a raise because we want your last week with us to be a happy one.'

Proverb: Old bosses never die – they just sit around on their assets.

The office boy was called into the manager's office and charged with telling lies about the organization. 'Now look here, Jimmy,' said the boss sternly, 'do you know what happens to boys who trifle with the truth?'

'Yes, sir,' said Jimmy. 'When they get old enough, you send them out as sales representatives.'

Sadly, the personnel manager had died, and an ambitious junior clerk went into the manager's office and said, 'Excuse me, sir, I was very sorry to hear that Mr Jones has died – but I wonder if I could possibly take his place?'

'It's all right with me,' said the boss. 'If you can arrange it with the undertaker.'

The boss was looking over his top salesman's expense accounts. 'What is this item here?' he asked. 'It seems a bit excessive.'

'Oh, that's my restaurant bill, sir,' said the salesman.

'Well, in future,' said the boss, 'don't buy any more restaurants!'

FIRST BOSS: 'I hear you're looking for a new Head Cashier.'

SECOND BOSS: 'That's right.'

FIRST BOSS: 'But didn't you just hire a new cashier last month?'

SECOND BOSS: 'Yes – that's the one we're looking for!'

One of our top industrialists had a large number of signs made up which consisted of only one word in very large letters: THINK. He stuck these up all over his factories and offices. He was never able to discover the identity of the employee who added the words OR THWIM to every sign at head office.

'Shall I put this memo to all staff up on the notice board, sir?' asked the secretary.

'No, put it on the office clock,' said the boss. 'I want everybody to see it.'

FIRST WORKER: 'How did the boss take it when you told him you were leaving next week?'

SECOND WORKER: 'He was furious! He thought it was this week!'

A young man barged into the manager's office and said breezily, 'Have you got an opening for a bright young man?'

'Yes, we have,' said the boss. 'Don't slam it on your way out.'

'Congratulations, sir,' said the young executive to the chairman of the board. 'Everyone at the stockholders' meeting was agreed that you gave a Rolls-Royce of a speech!'

'Why, thank you,' said the chairman, beaming.

'Yes, sir. They said you were well-oiled, almost inaudible and went on for a very long time.'

There were two candidates for the position of chairman of the board. One of them was pleading his case before the selection committee and he said, 'I have served this company faithfully for over thirty years, at great personal sacrifice to my health, my other interests, my wife and family, my . . .'

'Stop!' said a voice from the end of the table. 'You've done enough for us! I'm voting for the other fellow!'

A shady entrepreneur had made a fortune by wheeling and dealing but had never had a formal education. Some of his envious colleagues asked him how he had managed it. 'I just follow a few simple rules,' he said. 'For instance, I buy goods at £500 and sell them for £2,000 – and I'm quite happy with 3 per cent profit.'

The new boss had only been in the factory for three months but he had the distinct impression that all the workforce hated him. He called in the shop-floor manager and said, 'Why don't the men like me? At my last place, they gave me a set of silver-plated cutlery when I left.'

'Is that all?' said the manager. 'If you'd only leave here, we'd give you a solid gold dinner service!'

The chief buyer of a fashion house went into her boss's office to ask for a raise. 'Impossible!' said the boss. 'I'm already paying you more than any of the male executives and most of them have a wife and several children to support.'

'I was under the impression,' she said icily, 'that we got paid for what we produce at work – not what we produce at home.'

Two small-time businessmen, known for dealing in anything, met up. One of them said to the other in a confidential whisper: 'Would you like to buy an African elephant for £100?'

'Are you crazy?' said the second man. 'I live in a tower block and I've got four kids!'

'All right,' said the first man. 'Tell you what I'll do. I can let you have two African elephants for £150.'

'Ah!' said his friend. 'Now you're talking!'

'What is business ethics, Dad?' asked the young son of one of the bosses of a large clothing store.

'I'll give you an example,' said his father. 'A customer came in yesterday and bought some shirts. He paid with a £50 note and as I was putting it in the till I saw that he had given me two £50 notes stuck together. Now this is where business ethics come in. Should I tell my partner or not?'

The Lloyd's broker was somewhat annoyed when his application to join an exclusive business club was turned down. 'Never mind,' an acquaintance commiserated. 'They turned me down too. I got fifteen blackballs and there were only fourteen members on the selection committee. Apparently even the waiter didn't like me!'

A humble accountant came home from work in high spirits. 'Good news, dear,' he told his wife. 'The boss told me that he wants me to work in an advisory capacity, personally to him, at some time in the near future.'

'Did he really say that?' asked his wife disbelievingly.

'Well, not in so many words,' said her husband. 'He said, "When I want your advice, I'll ask for it."'

ASSISTANT MANAGER: 'But you can't fire me! Who are you going to get to fill my vacancy?'

MANAGER: 'Believe me, Sam, you're not leaving any vacancy!'

Efficiency expert: 'I'm pleased to see that you've taken on quite a few new employees since I installed my system.'

Manager: 'Yes, I had to hire them to take care of the system!'

'About my request for a raise,' said the assistant to his boss. 'I think you ought to know that three other companies are after me.'

'Oh, yes?' said the boss sceptically. 'What companies?'

'Gas, Electricity and Water,' replied the assistant.

A management committee has been defined as a group of the unqualified, appointed by the unwilling, to do the unnecessary.

Two business partners were having a heated argument about the expense accounts. 'Are you calling me a cheat?' yelled one. 'Have you ever heard my honesty questioned?'

'Questioned?' said the other partner. 'I've never even heard it mentioned!'

Two bosses met in a bank one morning. They had just concluded their business when a gang of masked men burst in. Their leader shouted, 'This is a hold-up! We want all the money in the safe – and you people hand over your wallets!'

One of the bosses whispered furtively to the other, 'Joe – you know that £100 I owe you? Well, here it is!'

The boss was complaining to his wife one evening. 'That new assistant of mine,' he said, 'is really one of the most incompetent and inefficient people I've ever had working for me.'

'Don't knock him,' said his wife. 'It's people like him who make you look good!'

A very powerful businessman had occasion to visit his doctor. After examining him, the doctor said, 'I'm sorry to tell you, you've got an ulcer.'

'Impossible!' roared the boss. 'I don't get ulcers! I give them!'

Boss to employee about to leave for a fortnight's vacation: 'Have a good time on your holiday, Briggs. Enjoy yourself, and when you come back, I've got something very serious to say to you.'

WIFE: 'Did you ask your boss for a raise today like I told you?'

HUSBAND: 'No, dear. I forgot in all the excitement of getting the sack.'

'I'm sorry we're having to let you go,' said the boss to his senior employee. 'But it may give you some satisfaction to know that the computer that's replacing you cost £100,000.'

'Why do you always employ married men in your office, dear?' asked the boss's wife one evening. 'What's wrong with bachelors?'

'Well,' explained the boss, 'married men don't get upset if I shout at them.'

Two business partners were playing golf one afternoon when one of them suddenly said, 'My God! We forgot to lock the office safe!'

'So what?' said the other. 'We're both here, aren't we?'

The Collector of Taxes recently received a letter from the boss of a car-hire firm which read: 'For the last three years, I have not declared all my profits and it's been preying on my conscience. I can't sleep nights. I enclose my cheque for £1,000. If I find I still can't sleep, I'll send you a cheque for the other £4,000.'

'I hear you have a special incentive plan here, sir,' said the new employee.

'That's right,' said the boss. 'We fire at the drop of a hat!'

A cashier in a large bank called over the manager and said, 'Sorry to bother you, sir, but this customer wants to cash a cheque for £50 and insists on having it all in 1p pieces.'

The manager looked at the customer and smiled politely. 'Certainly, sir,' he said. 'Any particular dates?'

The boss was welcoming his son into the business. 'I think you'll make a success of it,' he said. 'But don't imagine you're going to come in here and start at the top just because I'm your father. You'll begin as a partner, just like the rest of us did.'

'Look here, Jenkins,' said the boss to his assistant, as they met at the coffee machine, 'you're drinking far too much coffee. Caffeine is bad for you taken in excess – it can affect your work. Don't you know what the medical authorities say about coffee?'

'Yes, I do, sir,' said Jenkins. 'But I don't see what it's got to do with the stuff that comes out of this machine!'

A big business executive stepped out of his office and bumped into a group of colleagues. 'Coming to join us for lunch, Jack?' asked one.

'Sorry,' said the exec. 'I'm on the wagon!'

'**D**id you post those two parcels?' the boss asked the office boy one afternoon.

'Yes, I did, sir, but you'd put the wrong stamps on them.'

'What do you mean?' said the boss.

'Well, sir, you put stamps worth £7.50 on the local parcel and a 50p stamp on the one for Hong Kong. But don't worry, I soon put it right. I changed the addresses over.'

'You're late,' said the boss to his secretary when she strolled in at 10 a.m.

'I'm not really late, sir,' she said. 'I just took my coffee break before I came in.'

The sales manager of a large export firm received news one morning that one of his top salesmen had died in Milan. He immediately sent a fax to the Milan office: 'Return samples by airmail and search the body for orders.'

FIRST SECRETARY: 'Do you ever get nervous when you're alone with your boss in his office?'

SECOND SECRETARY: 'Yes, often! I'm always afraid he'll stop and ask me to take dictation!'

The seven-year-old son of the boss of a large advertising agency came home from Sunday School one day with a small printed religious tract. 'What have you got there?' asked his father.

'Nothing much,' said the boy. 'Just an ad about Heaven.'

A very attractive young lady called at the reception desk of a large business organization and asked to see the managing director. 'Certainly,' said the receptionist, and then added with a knowing smile, 'The boss is never so busy that he can't find time to see a pretty girl!'

'Good,' said the caller. 'Tell him his wife is here.'

Whenever they thought the manager was engaged, the four bank clerks played cards. One day he caught them at it. They didn't notice, so he decided to teach them a lesson. He rang the fire alarm four times, but the clerks ignored the bell and carried on playing. Two minutes later, the barman from the pub next door walked in with four pints of beer.

The boss was interviewing a young woman for a job. In an effort to impress him with her intelligence, she said, 'Among other things, I'm very good at doing difficult crossword puzzles – in fact, I've won many prizes.'

'That's very interesting,' said the boss, 'but I'm looking for someone who can be smart during office hours.'

'Oh,' said the young lady, 'this was during office hours!'

Boss: 'We can offer a private pension scheme, six weeks' paid holiday, bonus payments, a company car, mortgage assistance and free health insurance.'

Applicant: 'Sounds fine. What's the salary?'

Boss: 'Good Lord, you don't expect a salary as well, do you?'

The boss invariably held his staff meetings at 4.30 on Friday afternoons. 'Isn't that rather an inconvenient time?' asked one of his colleagues one day at lunch.

'Not at all,' replied the boss. 'I find it most convenient. Nobody ever wants to get into a long argument with me.'

A rough guide to those cryptic notes from your boss:

'See me and give me the benefit of your thinking of this.' ['I'm not taking the can for this one on my own.']

'For your consideration.' ['I can't make head or tail of it.']

'Please note and initial.' ['If anything goes wrong, we're all in this together.']

'Let's take a survey among senior management.' ['I haven't a clue what we should do – let someone else decide.']

'Will you take a look at this and let me have an in-depth report in due course.' ['If we can stall for long enough, perhaps everybody will forget all about it.']

The chief accountant advised his assistant always to add up any column of figures at least three times before showing him the result. The following day, the assistant came into his office with a sheet of calculations and said, 'Here you are, sir – I've added these figures up ten times.'

'Excellent!' said the chief accountant.

'And here are the ten answers,' added his assistant.